PEARSON

ALWAYS LEARNING

Ice Island 4

ACTIVITY BOOK

Contents

T0345708

WELCOME

1 (1:03) **Listen and say.**

1. telescope
2. goggles
3. wet suit
4. clock
5. radio
6. skis
7. submarine
8. flippers

2 (1:04) **Listen, find and number the objects.**

3 **Read, look and write.**

1 ___The radio___ is ___on___ the chair.
2 _____ next to the desk.
3 The clock is _____.
4 The flippers _____ under _____.

4 Read and write *F* (Finn), *D* (Dylan) or *J* (Jenny).

Finn

Dylan

Jenny

1 He's got glasses. `D`
2 She's smiling. ☐
3 He likes snowboarding. ☐
4 She's got a bag. ☐

5 He's wearing boots and a hat. ☐
6 She's wearing a skirt. ☐
7 He's wearing a coat and a scarf. ☐
8 They're boys. ☐☐

5 (1:05) Look, listen and say.

1  It's quarter to five.

2  It's quarter past five.

6 Ask and answer.

A: What's the time?   **B:** It's quarter past eight.

1   **2**   **3**   **4**  **5**   **6**

1 Friends

1 Find and circle six words.

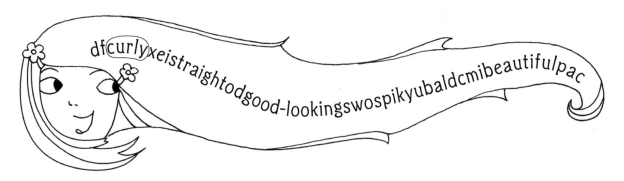

dfcurlyxeistraightodgood-lookingswospikyubaldcmibeautifulpac

2 Look and write words from Activity 1.

1 I've got ____curly____ hair.

Emma

2 I've got _____ hair.

Maddy

3 I've got _____ hair.

Robbie

4 I'm _____ .

Dan

3 Find and write the questions.

1　does　look　what　she　like　　_What does she look like?_

2　look　what　do　like　they　　_____

3　look　does　he　what　like　　_____

4 Read and choose. Then look and tick (✓) the true sentences.

a

1　She **has got** / **is** beautiful. ☐
2　She **has got** / **is** glasses. ☐

c

b

1　He **is** / **has got** bald. ✓
2　He **is** / **has got** long hair. ☐

1　They **are** / **have got** tall. ☐
2　They **are** / **have got** curly hair. ☐

5 Match the questions in Activity 3 with the pictures in Activity 4.

1　_b_　　　　2　☐　　　　3　☐

6 🔊 1:09 Listen and complete.

	Dad	Mum	Grandad
hair	_bald_		
eyes			
other	_tall_		

7 Write sentences about the people in Activity 6 in your notebook.

Dad's tall and bald. He's got ...

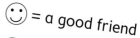

8 Read and match.

1 She's got a lot of friends because
2 She's got a lot of friends but
3 She's got a lot of friends and

a she hasn't got brothers or sisters.
b she's got a lot of pets.
c she's funny and kind.

4 I'm tall because
5 I'm tall but
6 I'm tall and

d I've got straight black hair.
e my mum and dad are tall.
f I'm not two metres tall!

9 Complete the words.

What makes a good friend?

1 This person is g _o_ _o_ d–lo _o_ _k_ _i_ ng. ☺ ☺ ☹
2 This person is k __ __ d. ☺ ☺ ☹
3 This person is c __ __ ve __. ☺ ☺ ☹
4 This person isn't f __ __ n y. ☺ ☺ ☹
5 This person is b o s __ __. ☺ ☺ ☹
6 This person is s __ y. ☺ ☺ ☹
7 This person isn't __ __ __ r t y. ☺ ☺ ☹
8 This person is l __ z __. ☺ ☺ ☹

? ? ?

☺ = a good friend
☺ = don't mind
☹ = a bad friend

10 What makes a good friend? Read and choose in Activity 9.

11 Write about your good friend.

SEARCH

My Friend

Tell us about your friend!

_____ is _____ and _____.

He/She's _____ but I don't mind.

He/She's my friend because _____.

SUBMIT ▶

12 (1:13) **Say and complete. Then listen and check.**

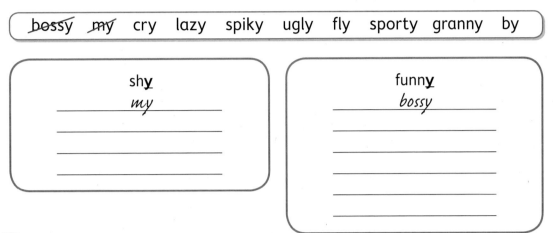

| bossy | ~~my~~ | cry | lazy | spiky | ugly | fly | sporty | granny | by |

sh**y**

_my_ _____

_____

_____

_____

funn**y**

bossy _____

_____

_____

_____

_____

_____

_____

13 (1:14) **Listen. Where is Carlos? Is he happy?**

14 (1:15) **Listen again and match.**

1   Megan is

2   The mum and dad are

3   The food is

a   short.
b   nice.
c   funny.
d   kind.
e   bossy.

15 **Imagine you are staying with this family in Britain. Look and write to a friend.**

| bossy | good | tall | straight | kind | curly | nice | spiky | bad |

Emily   Steven

●●○   **From:** _____

To: _____

Subject: My stay in Britain!

Dear _____

I'm having a _____ time here in Britain.

Emily is _____

She's got _____

Steven is _____

He's got _____

Their mum is _____

She's got _____

Love,

_____

16 Look and write.

Doctor Al   ~~Rufus~~   Captain Formosa   Ivan

 ①    ②    ③    ④

Rufus

17 Find and write.

_Wh_

18 Look, think and complete. Then add two more.

~~sun~~

cloud   lion   ~~water~~

frog   fire

warm colours	cool colours
sun	water
_____	_____
_____	_____
_____	_____

19 (1:17) Look, listen and choose.

These pictures are by an artist called Dürer. The pictures are of the artist.

a

b

20 Find and write the questions. Then answer about Picture a.

he ~~how~~ look old does what is like he

1 _How_____   _He_____

2 _____   _____

21 Read and write.

Talking about appearance

What	¹ _do_ I **do** you ² _____ he/she/it **do** we **do** they	look ³ _____ ?	

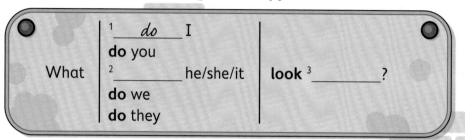

I'm not very clever but I'm sporty and I'm good-looking.

I like you because you're funny!

22 🔘 1:18 Read and write. Then listen and check.

From:	maddy6819@246.com
To:	jasmine397@2561.com
Subject:	My new life!

Hi, Jasmine!

Thanks for your email. I like my new home ¹ _but_ I'm sad ² _____ you aren't here with me.

My new friends, Emma, Robbie and Dan, ³ _____ very kind.

Emma's ⁴ _____ straight brown hair ⁵ _____ brown eyes. She's very pretty.

What ⁶ _____ you look like now? ⁷ _____ you got long hair or short hair? And what ⁸ _____ your new friend, Caitlin, look like? Send me a photo!

Lots of love,

Maddy

23 Look and complete.

~~bald~~ straight hair
long hair   beautiful
tall   spiky hair
blue eyes   good-looking

am/is/are	have/has got
bald	

24 **Read and write.**

- Describe your favourite person at home or your favourite teacher at school.
- Use: *He's/She's . . .*; *He's/She's got . . .*

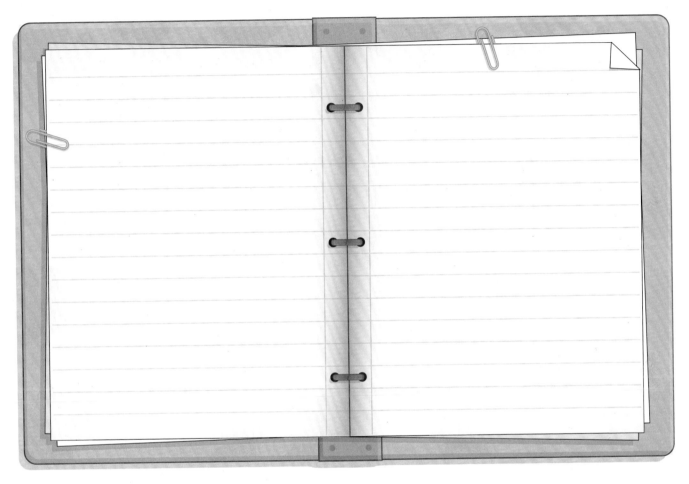

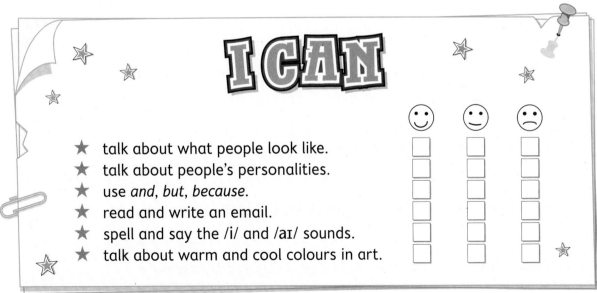

I CAN

☺ ☺ ☹

★ talk about what people look like.
★ talk about people's personalities.
★ use *and, but, because.*
★ read and write an email.
★ spell and say the /i/ and /aɪ/ sounds.
★ talk about warm and cool colours in art.

2 My life

1 **Read and match.**

| 1 get | g | 3 make | ☐ | 5 go | ☐ | 7 do | ☐ |
| 2 brush | ☐ | 4 tidy | ☐ | 6 meet | ☐ | 8 wash | ☐ |

a my homework   **c** my room   **e** my friends   **g** up
b my teeth   **d** my face   **f** my bed   **h** to bed

2 (1:22) **Look and write. Then listen and tick (✓) or cross (✗) for Dan.**

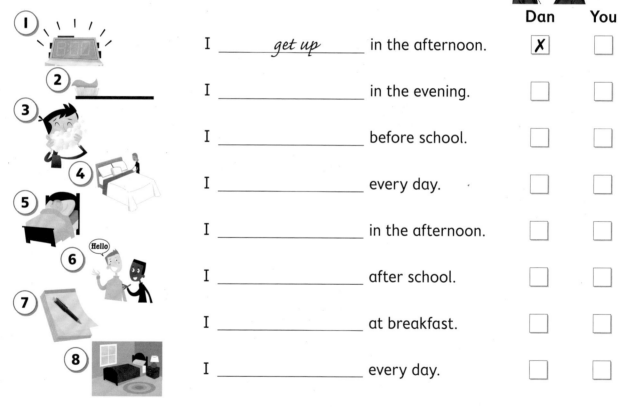

	Dan	You
1 I ___get up___ in the afternoon.	✗	☐
2 I _____ in the evening.	☐	☐
3 I _____ before school.	☐	☐
4 I _____ every day.	☐	☐
5 I _____ in the afternoon.	☐	☐
6 I _____ after school.	☐	☐
7 I _____ at breakfast.	☐	☐
8 I _____ every day.	☐	☐

3 **Tick (✓) or cross (✗) the sentences for you.**

4 **Correct the sentences with a cross (✗) in your notebook.**

I don't get up in the afternoon. I get up in the morning.

5 Find and circle seven words. Then complete.

y o u r h i s t h e i r i t s h e r o u r m y

1 I → _____
2 you → _____ *your* _____
3 he → _____
4 she → _____
5 it → _____
6 we → _____
7 they → _____

6 Read and choose.

At half past eight every day, Dan and ¹***their /*** (***his***) friend, Maddy, go to school by bus. But today there's a problem. It's nine o'clock and ²***their / its*** bus isn't here!

Dan: Let's go to school by bike.
Maddy: I can't ride ³***her / my*** bike. It's only got one of ⁴***his / its*** wheels.
Dan: My sister's got a bike. Ride that!
Maddy: But ⁵***your / her*** sister is eighteen. ⁶***Their / Her*** bike is very big.
Dan: Look! It's OK. ⁷***Our / His*** bus is here now!

7 (1:24) What do they do on Saturdays? Listen and match.

1 Robbie and Emma   a do/homework
2 Their mum and dad   b tidy/room
3 Maddy   c read/books in bed
4 Dan   d play/favourite computer games

8 (1:25) Listen again. Write sentences in your notebook.

1 Robbie and Emma don't tidy their rooms on Saturdays.
  They play their favourite computer games.

2 Their mum and dad …

9 **Look and write.**

always   usually   often   sometimes   never (×2)

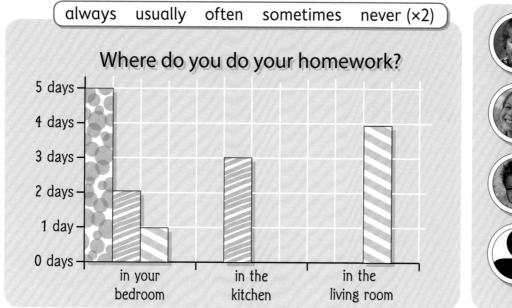

Where do you do your homework?

Matt

Sasha

Jamie

You

1 Matt ___*never*___ does his homework in the kitchen.

2 Sasha _____ does her homework in the kitchen.

3 Matt _____ does his homework in his bedroom.

4 Sasha and Matt _____ do their homework in the living room.

5 Sasha _____ does her homework in her bedroom.

6 Jamie _____ does his homework in the living room.

10 **Complete the chart for you. Write sentences in your notebook.**

I usually do my homework in my bedroom.

11 **Find and write.**

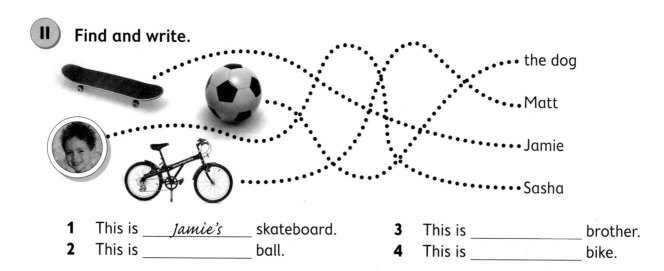

the dog

Matt

Jamie

Sasha

1 This is ___*Jamie's*___ skateboard.
2 This is _____ ball.

3 This is _____ brother.
4 This is _____ bike.

12 Write the correct form of the words in brackets.

a He _____goes_____ (go) to school.
b She _____ (watch) TV.
c He _____ (make) his bed.
d She _____ (wash) her face.
e She _____ (do) her homework.
f He _____ (brush) his hair.

13 (1:30) Count and write the number of syllables in the new words. Listen, check and say.

a [1]   **b** [ ]   **c** [ ]   **d** [ ]   **e** [ ]   **f** [ ]

14 (1:31) Listen and write.

I don't like mornings. My big brother
¹_____always_____ gets up at five o'clock
because he's a farmer. He washes
his face and makes his breakfast.
He ²_____ sings songs in
the morning. ³_____ songs
are horrible. I can't sleep after that.
I ⁴_____ get up at six o'clock
because I'm hungry. I like eggs for
breakfast but I ⁵_____ eat
toast. Why? Because my brother eats
⁶_____ eggs at half past five.
Grrr!

15 Complete for you.

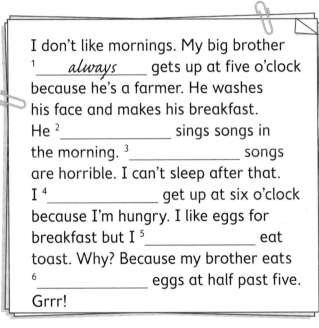

My Saturday morning

Time	Activity
	get up
	have breakfast

16 Write about your Saturday morning in your notebook.

On saturday morning,
I usually get up at
nine o'clock. I ...

17 **Read and choose.**

1 Captain Formosa always **get** / **gets** up at six.
2 Then he has **his** / **my** breakfast.
3 He **gives** / **eats** some fish to the penguins.
4 He **read** / **reads** his map.
5 **It's** / **He's** a treasure map of Ice Island.
6 The map **aren't** / **isn't** here.

18 **Look and write.**

> meet his friends   go swimming   ~~have lunch~~
> go to bed   tidy his room   have dinner

He has lunch at half past twelve.

19 **Look at page 8. Find and write.**

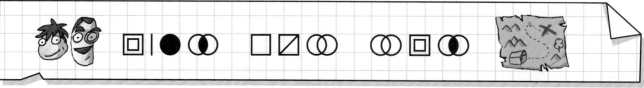

Ivan and Rufus

20 Read and circle. *True* (✓) or *false* (✗)? Then find and write the answer.

Health Quiz

		✓	✗
1	Milk is good for your teeth and bones.	(B)	M
2	A healthy person never eats fruit or vegetables.	E	O
3	Riding a bike isn't healthy.	A	N
4	Cake isn't very good for you.	E	T
5	An apple – only an apple – is a good, healthy breakfast.	Y	S

What's my name?

B _ _ _ _ _ !

21 (1:34) Listen, read and find eight differences. Listen again and correct.

★ MUDCHESTER UNITED ★

Application form

We want healthy football players for Mudchester United.
Write about your day.

I get up at ~~seven~~ *ten* o'clock. I have eggs on toast for breakfast

and a drink of orange juice. I always brush my teeth after

breakfast. I go to the swimming pool in the afternoon.

I often play football after dinner. After that, I wash my face

and I go to bed at nine o'clock.

22 Read and write.

Possessive adjectives

I brush **my** hair.
You tidy ¹_____*your*_____ room.
He makes ²_____ bed.
She meets **her** friends.
It washes ³_____ face.
We do **our** homework.
They brush ⁴_____ teeth.

Oh, Bill! You never tidy the living room.

Sorry, Mum!

23 Read and choose.

Lucy and Lily are ¹**sister's** /(**sisters**).
Lucy often does ²**his / her** homework in
³**Lily / Lily's** bedroom because Lily has got
a computer. In the afternoon, they meet
⁴**they / their** friends at the park. Lucy has
got a skateboard. ⁵**Lily / Lucy** sometimes
goes on ⁶**Lily's / Lucy's** skateboard. Watch
out, Lily!

24 Read again and write. *True* or *false*?

1 Lucy has got a computer. _____*False*_____
2 Lucy often does her homework on the computer. _____
3 They meet their friends in the morning. _____
4 Lily always goes on Lucy's skateboard. _____

25 **Read and write.**

- Write sentences about what you do in the evening.
  Use: *I always/usually/often/sometimes/never . . .*
- Ask a friend and write sentences about him or her.

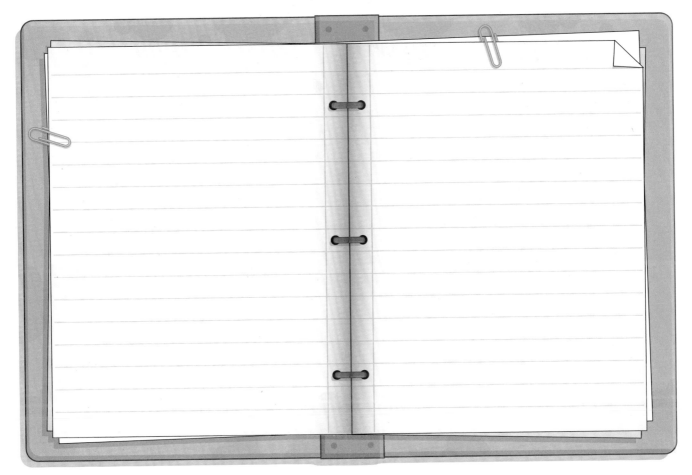

I CAN

	☺	☺	☹
★ talk about my daily routine.	☐	☐	☐
★ use *my, your, his, her, its, our, their.*	☐	☐	☐
★ use *'s.*	☐	☐	☐
★ say how often I do things.	☐	☐	☐
★ read and understand a questionnaire.	☐	☐	☐
★ spell and say the /z/ and /ɪz/ sounds.	☐	☐	☐
★ talk about healthy/unhealthy foods and habits.	☐	☐	☐

3 Free time

1 Complete the words and match. Then draw the missing picture.

 a

 b

 c

1 c _l_ _i_ m b i n g
2 th ___ ___ w i n g
3 ___ ___ t t i n g
4 c ___ ___ c h i n g
5 d ___ v ___ n g
6 k ___ ___ k i n g

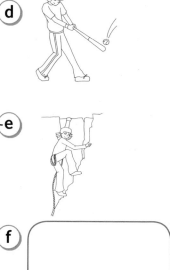 d

e

f

2 Look and write.

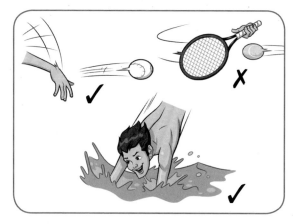

Robbie

1 I'm good at _____ _throwing._ _____
2 I'm not good at _____.
3 I'm good at _____.

Dan

4 I'm good at _____.
5 I'm not good at _____.
6 I'm good at _____.

3 1:39 Listen and say who is talking.

4 (1:41) **Look and write. Then listen and check.**

are   they're   ~~I'm~~   at   isn't   am   good

1 ¹ *I'm* good
² _____ throwing.

He ³ _____ good at catching.

³ _____
⁴ _____ you
⁵ _____ at climbing?

Yes, I ⁶ _____ but ⁷ _____ good at jumping!

5 **Look and write questions. Then ask a friend and choose.**

1 _____ *Are you good at kicking?* _____   Yes, I am. / No, I'm not.

2 _____   Yes, I am. / No, I'm not.

3 _____   Yes, I am. / No, I'm not.

4 _____   Yes, I am. / No, I'm not.

5 _____   Yes, I am. / No, I'm not.

6 _____   Yes, I am. / No, I'm not.

7 _____   Yes, I am. / No, I'm not.

6 **Write about your friend in your notebook.**

Charlie is good at kicking and sailing but he isn't good at climbing and diving.

7 Complete the crossword. Then find and write.

SONG

I love _s_ _ _ _ _ _ _ _ _ !

1 | s | k | a | t | e | b | o | a | r | d | i | n | g |

2 | | | l | | | | | | | | | | |

3 | | | | | y | | | | | | | | |

4 | | | | | | | | | | s | |

5 | t | | | | | | | | |

6 | | | c | | |

7 | | | a | | | |

8 Look and write.

1 _He loves trampolining._

2 _____

3 _____

4 _____

5 _____

6 _____

🏆 = is/are good at

♥ = loves/love

😖 = doesn't/ don't like

9 🔊 1:44 Find and write. Then listen and answer for Robbie.

1 (like) (you) (do) (doing) (what)   2 (at) (you) (good) (are) (what)

What _____   _____

_I_ _____   _____

10 **Read. Is Ellie good at doing sport?**

Dear Granny,
Action Camp is great! I'm here with Ellie because we both love doing sports. We go swimming every morning. I love swimming. I can swim 15 metres underwater now. We have diving lessons, too. I'm not very good at diving because I feel scared but Ellie can dive from the big diving board. She's fantastic! Ellie and I like trampolining after lunch and we love playing tennis together in the afternoon. Ellie's very good at running and hitting the ball.
Lots of love,
Mark

11 **Read and answer.**

1   What does Mark do in the morning?   _Mark goes swimming in the morning._
2   Can Mark swim?   _____
3   Is Mark good at diving?   _____
4   Is Ellie good at diving?   _____
5   What do they like doing after lunch?   _____
6   Do they like playing tennis?   _____

12 **Look and complete. Write the -ing forms.**

kick   surf   swim   run   dance   rollerblade   fish
trampoline   paint   dive   ride   sail   throw   hit

+ ing	
kick	kicking
_____	_____
_____	_____
_____	_____

+ last letter + ing	
swim	swimming
_____	_____
_____	_____
_____	_____

- e + ing	
dance	dancing
_____	_____
_____	_____
_____	_____

13 **Imagine you're at a camp. Write a letter to a friend in your notebook.**

Dear Lucy,
I'm at Beach Camp this week. I love ...

14 Read and choose. *True* or *false*?

1 Finn is with Dylan and Holly.   *True /* (*False*)
2 Finn and Dylan have got radios.   *True / False*
3 Ivan and Rufus are reading the map.   *True / False*
4 Finn isn't watching polar bears.   *True / False*
5 Finn is good at stopping.   *True / False*

15 Look, read and answer.

Are they good at running?
Yes, they are.

Is he good at diving?

Can he ride a bike?

Do they like skiing?

16 Look at page 8. Find and write.

17 (1:51) **Read and write. Then listen and check.**

> write   writing   play   playing
> good   at   ~~my~~   sometimes

Hi. ¹_____My_____ name's David. I have guitar lessons every week. I love ²_____ the guitar – my teacher is great. My friend, Melissa, is ³_____ singing and her brother can ⁴_____ the drums. We ⁵_____ play songs together. It's fun! I like ⁶_____ music, too. One day, I want to ⁷_____ music for films.

18 (1:52) **Listen to the music and tick (✓) for you.**

1	cool ☐	OK ☐	bad ☐
2	cool ☐	OK ☐	bad ☐
3	cool ☐	OK ☐	bad ☐
4	cool ☐	OK ☐	bad ☐

5	cool ☐	OK ☐	bad ☐
6	cool ☐	OK ☐	bad ☐
7	cool ☐	OK ☐	bad ☐
8	cool ☐	OK ☐	bad ☐

19 (1:53) **Listen again and choose your favourite. Then find that number and read about you.**

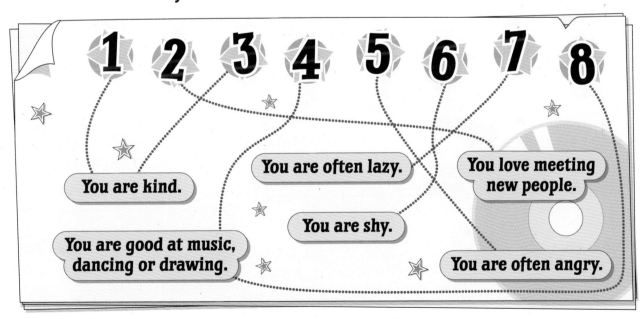

1 2 3 4 5 6 7 8

You are kind.

You are often lazy.

You love meeting new people.

You are shy.

You are good at music, dancing or drawing.

You are often angry.

20 Read and write.

Talking about abilities

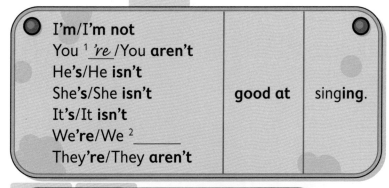

I love singing!

But he isn't *good* at singing!

21 1:54 Look and write. Then listen and choose. *True* or *false*?

= is/are good at
= loves/love
✔ = can
✗ = can't
= doesn't/don't like

1 Sam ♡ 🎸

_____Sam loves playing the guitar._____ (**True**)/ **False**

2 Anna ✗ ♟ _____ **True / False**

3 The children 🏆 🎤 _____ **True / False**

4 Rick 😣 🛹 _____ **True / False**

5 Jo and Flo ✔ 🛼 _____ **True / False**

6 Bill 😣 🎨 _____ **True / False**

22 **Read and write.**

- Write about your abilities, likes and dislikes.
- Use: *I'm good at* -ing; *I like/don't like* -ing.

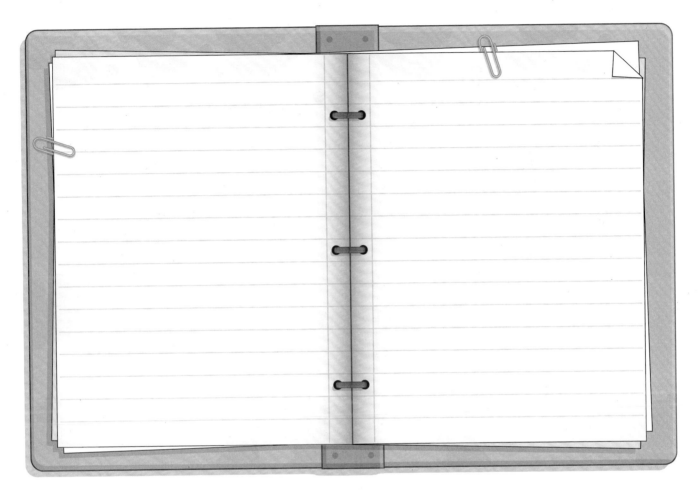

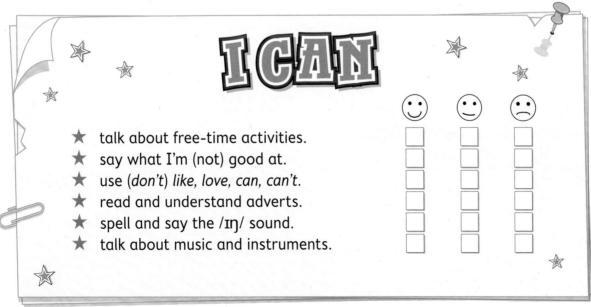

★ talk about free-time activities.
★ say what I'm (not) good at.
★ use (*don't*) *like, love, can, can't*.
★ read and understand adverts.
★ spell and say the /ɪŋ/ sound.
★ talk about music and instruments.

1 Complete the words.

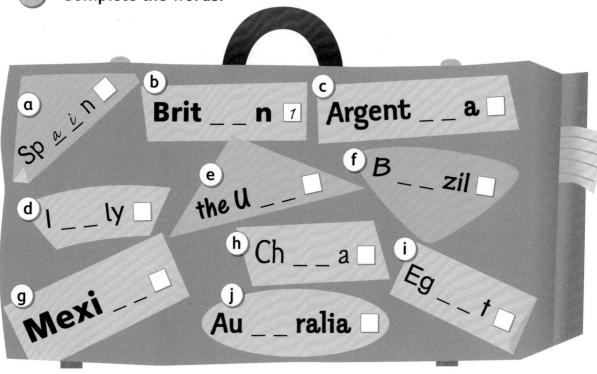

a. Sp _a_ _i_ n ☐

b. **Brit _ _ n** [1]

c. **Argent _ _ a** ☐

d. I _ _ ly ☐

e. the U _ _ _ ☐

f. B _ _ zil ☐

g. **Mexi _ _** ☐

h. Ch _ _ a ☐

i. Eg _ _ t ☐

j. Au _ _ ralia ☐

2 (2:03) Listen and number the countries in order.

3 Complete the crossword with words from Activity 1.

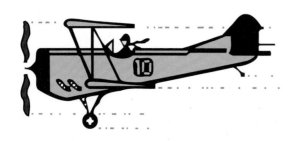

Crossword:
- A u s t r a l i a z (down)
- A _ _ _ x _ _ _
- _ _ _ h
- _ y _
- r g _ _ _
- a u
- _ s _ _
- y

4 **2:05** **Listen and draw.**

5 **Read and write *a*, *some* or *any*.**

1 There are _____some_____ long rivers in the USA.
2 There isn't _____ rainforest in Italy.
3 There aren't _____ giraffes in Britain.
4 There are _____ old houses in Spain.
5 There's _____ big waterfall in Brazil and Argentina.

6 **Look and write.**

1 hippos/China ✗
   _____There aren't any hippos in China._____
2 a rainforest/Australia ✓
   _____
3 a snowy mountain/Egypt ✗
   _____
4 elephants/Mexico ✗
   _____
5 beautiful beaches/Spain ✓
   _____

7 **Write about your country in your notebook.**

There are some pretty beaches in my country.

8 Find and circle eight words. Then find and write the answer.

A p y r a m i d u s f o r e s t d e s e r t t r v o l c a n o a l a k e c i t y l s t a t u e i c a v e a

Where are they going?

A _____

9 Look and complete. Use words from Activity 8.

			Britain	Spain
1		_lake_ s	✓	✓
2		_____ es	✗	✓
3		a big _____	✓	✓
4		_____ s	✓	✓
5		a big _____	✗	✗
6		_____ s	✓	✓
7		a _____	✗	✓
8		a _____	✓	✓

10 Look at Activity 9. Write questions and answers in your notebook.

1 Are there any lakes in Britain? Yes, there are.

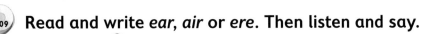

11 (2:09) **Read and write *ear*, *air* or *ere*. Then listen and say.**

¹Wh_*e r e*_ is Claire?
She's ²th_____, on the ³ch_____.
She's ⁴w_____ing a dress and a
⁵b_____ in her ⁶h_____.

12 (2:10) **Listen. Which country is Mia in now?**

13 (2:11) **Listen again and choose.**

1 Mia is talking to her *grandad* / *granny*.
2 She's in a *rainforest* / *city*.
3 There are some *beaches* / *pyramids* in Rio.
4 There's a big *island* / *statue*, too.
5 Brazilian people are good at *dancing* / *singing*.

14 (2:12) **Read and write. Then listen and check.**

rainforest   lake   trees   animals   beautiful   ~~Grandad~~

Dear ¹ _Grandad_ ,
Hello from the Amazon ² _____
in Brazil! There are a lot of tall green
³ _____ in the rainforest and some
dangerous ⁴ _____ , too! I'm fishing
in a ⁵ _____ today. I can see some
monkeys! It's very ⁶ _____ here.
Lots of love,
Mia

Mr Tracy
15 Warwick Close
Upton, PV17 3BP
Britain

15 **Think about your favourite holiday. Write a postcard in your notebook.**

Dear Matt,
*   I'm having a great time here in the USA. There are …*

16 **Read and correct.**

1 Captain Formosa's got the map.

Captain Formosa hasn't got the map.

2 The Captain's got a good memory.

_____

3 There are some pyramids on Ice Island.

_____

4 The treasure's under a volcano.

_____

5 There's a cave in Snow Lake.

_____

17 (2:14) **Listen and circle the correct penguin.**

18 **Look at page 8. Find and write.**

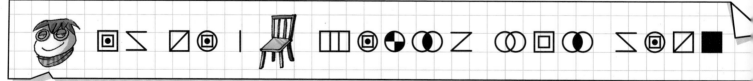

19 Listen and write.

Come to Greenland!

¹ _Ride_ on snowmobiles!

Climb snowy ² _____!

See ³ _____ and waterfalls of ice!

There aren't ⁴ _____ big cities here but there are ⁵ _____ beautiful polar ⁶ _____ and reindeer in this cold place. Every ⁷ _____ in Greenland is an adventure!

Greenland – a world of ice!

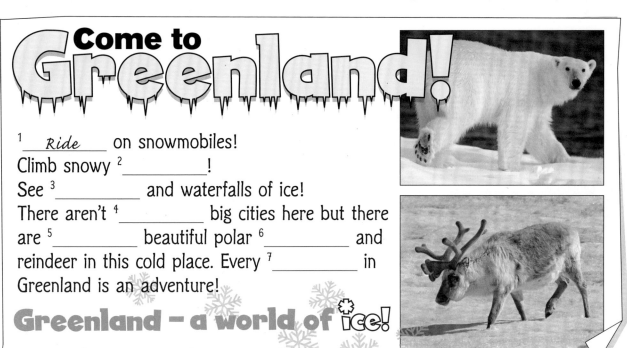

20 Read and choose.

Is a holiday in Greenland right for you?

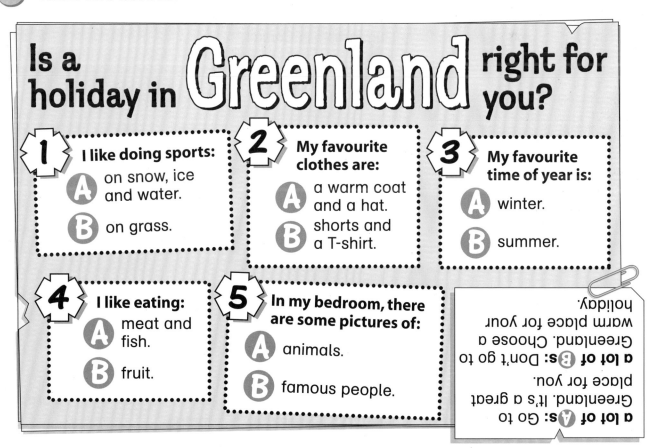

1 I like doing sports:
- **A** on snow, ice and water.
- **B** on grass.

2 My favourite clothes are:
- **A** a warm coat and a hat.
- **B** shorts and a T-shirt.

3 My favourite time of year is:
- **A** winter.
- **B** summer.

4 I like eating:
- **A** meat and fish.
- **B** fruit.

5 In my bedroom, there are some pictures of:
- **A** animals.
- **B** famous people.

a lot of A s: Go to Greenland. It's a great place for you.

a lot of B s: Don't go to Greenland. Choose a warm place for your holiday.

21 Read and write.

a, some and any

There's ¹ __a__ lake.
There isn't ² _____ forest.
There are ³ _____ cities.
There aren't ⁴ _____ statues.

Is there ⁵ _____ statue? | Yes, there is.
No, there isn't.

Are there ⁶ _____ caves? | Yes, there are.
No, there aren't.

Are there any pyramids?

Yes, there are!

22 Read and write the questions. Then listen and write the answers.

1 ___Are there any___ big forests in China?
___Yes, there are.___

2 _____ desert in China?
_____

3 _____ caves in China?
_____

4 _____ pyramids in China?
_____

5 _____ nice statues in China?
_____

6 _____ lions in China?
_____

23 Listen again and choose.

1 The boy (wants) / doesn't want to go to China.
2 The desert is called the Gobi / Moby Desert.
3 In China, some people live / work in caves.
4 The pyramids of China are / aren't famous.
5 There are statues of horses / camels.

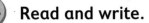 **Read and write.**

- Write about a place you know.
- Use: *There's a . . .*; *There isn't a . . .*; *There are some . . .*; *There aren't any . . .*

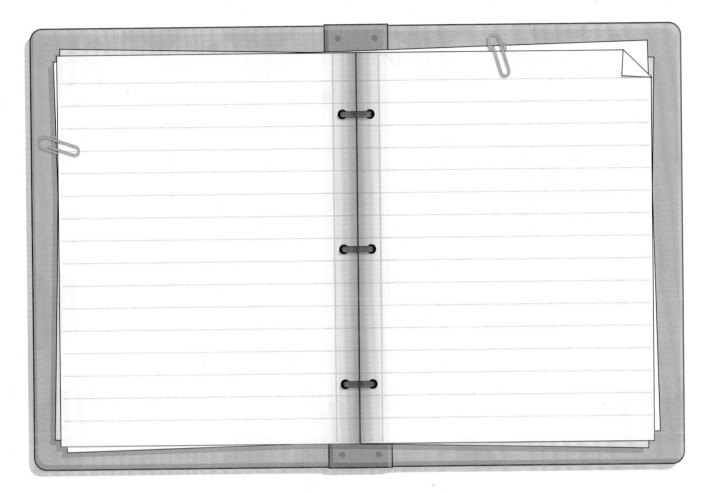

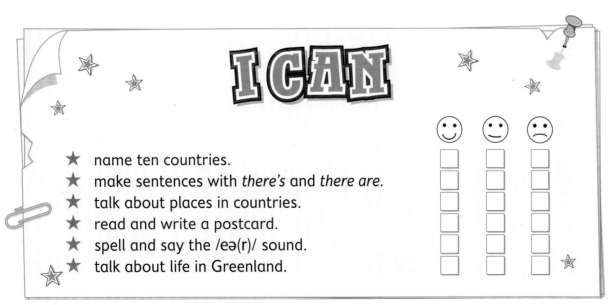

I CAN

	☺	☺	☹
★ name ten countries.	□	□	□
★ make sentences with *there's* and *there are*.	□	□	□
★ talk about places in countries.	□	□	□
★ read and write a postcard.	□	□	□
★ spell and say the /eə(r)/ sound.	□	□	□
★ talk about life in Greenland.	□	□	□

5 Shopping

1 Find and circle.

s	w	i	m	s	u	i	t	c
a	d	j	d	u	j	l	o	o
t	r	a	i	n	e	r	s	a
s	s	c	w	g	a	h	a	t
o	j	k	g	l	n	v	n	s
c	e	e	h	a	s	s	d	c
k	a	t	g	s	s	h	a	a
s	h	o	e	s	u	i	l	r
g	l	o	v	e	s	r	s	f
s	d	r	e	s	s	t	e	g

2 Look and write. Use *is/are* and words from Activity 1.

1 How much ___is___ that ___swimsuit___?

2 How much _____ those _____?

3 How much _____ that _____?

4 How much _____ those _____?

3 🔊 2:22 Listen. What does Maddy buy?

4 Look and write the prices in words.

BIKE **1** £1000

T-SHIRT **2** • £21.50

SKATEBOARD **3**

£99

4 £122

SUNGLASSES

TRAINERS **5** £420

SANDALS £55.50 **6**

1 _____*a thousand pounds*_____
2 _____
3 _____
4 _____
5 _____
6 _____

5 (2:25) The prices in Activity 4 are wrong. Listen and choose.

1 **a** £990	**b** £999	**c** £919
2 **a** £12.50	**b** £20.50	**c** £15.20
3 **a** £9.50	**b** £19.50	**c** £90.50
4 **a** £12	**b** £20	**c** £21
5 **a** £40.20	**b** £42.20	**c** £42
6 **a** £26.50	**b** £25.50	**c** £25.55

6 (2:26) Read and write. Then listen and check.

course   hundred   ~~much~~   please   pounds   how

David: Hello. How ¹ _____*much*_____ are those gloves, please?
Shop assistant: They're four ² _____ fifty.
David: And ³ _____ much are those shorts?
Shop assistant: They're a ⁴ _____ pounds.
David: Oh . . . can I buy these gloves, ⁵ _____?
Shop assistant: Yes, of ⁶ _____.

NEW!

Lesson 2   37

7 Complete the words and match.

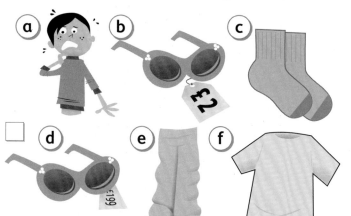

1 c h _e_ _a_ p sunglasses [_b_]

2 d __ __ k grey socks [ ]

3 a l __ __ __ h t grey T-shirt [ ]

4 e x __ __ __ __ s __ v __ sunglasses [ ]

5 b __ g g __ jeans [ ]

6 a t __ g __ t jumper [ ]

8 Look and write.

| dark tight expensive baggy |

1 _____
   They're too tight.

2 It's _____

3 _____

4 I can't see!
   _____

9 Write about your clothes in your notebook. Use *too*.

| long short old baggy big |
| small tight dark light |

My green jumper is too tight.

10 (2:30) **Look and write *ight* or *ite*. Then listen and say.**

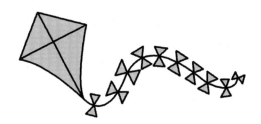

My new ¹k___*ite*___ isn't dark.
It's ²l_____.

The moon is ³wh_____ at ⁴n_____.

The ⁵firef_____er's
jacket is too ⁶t_____.

Do you use your ⁷r_____ hand
when you ⁸wr_____?

11 (2:31) **Listen and tick (✓) the adverts the boys talk about.**

¹**BIKE**, blue, for a boy
160 cm tall, £123.
Tel: 08459 2652741 ✓

²**COMPUTER
GAMES**, twenty
children's games, £17.
gamer@yoho.it.uk ☐

³**SCARF**, £6.50,
red and white.
footballfan@
bkinternet.co.uk ☐

⁴**SKATEBOARD**,
new, £38.
Tel: 08459 4839223 ☐

⁵**DOG**, six years old, black,
good with children, wants a
new home.
Tel: 08459 3221345 ☐

⁶**JACKET**, £25, white, for a
four-year-old girl.
whiteshop@intweb.com ☐

12 (2:32) **Listen again and write.**

1 The bike in the advert is too ___*big*___.
2 The skateboard is too _____.
3 Tom's mum doesn't like _____.
4 Tom wants to buy the _____.

13 **Write three adverts. Then
look at your friend's adverts
and talk about them.**

> I want a toy robot but
> £20 is too expensive.

14 **Read and answer.**

    1 Where are Jenny, Finn and Dylan?   *They're in a shop.*

    2 How do Finn and Dylan feel?

    3 Who is in the changing room?

    4 What are they wearing?

    5 Do the children catch the thieves?

    6 How do the thieves get away?

15 2:34 **Listen and write the prices. What does Jenny buy?**

16 **Look at page 8. Find and write.**

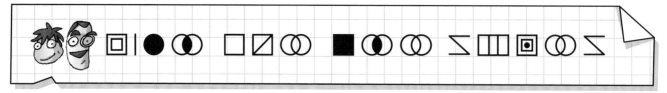

17 **Read and write.**

> Sailing shoes   ~~Trousers and a T-shirt~~   Sunglasses
> A warm jacket   A swimsuit

Winderton Sailing School

Clothes list for sailing lessons

1 _____Trousers and a T-shirt_____
Don't wear your favourite clothes. Choose something old and not too expensive.

2 _____
At sea, it's often too windy for summer clothes, even on sunny days.

3 _____
The sunlight on the water is very bad for your eyes.

4 _____
Our boats are too wet for trainers or sandals.

5 _____
After the lessons, you can dive from the boat and have fun in the water.

18 (2:35) **Listen and complete.**

	Activity	Clothes
	1 _____sailing_____	2warm _____ 3 _____ 4 _____
	5 _____	6 _____ 7 _____ 8 _____ trousers
	9 _____	10long _____ 11 _____ 12 _____

19 **Think of an activity and make a list. Your friend guesses the activity.**

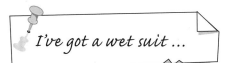

I've got a wet suit ...

20 Read and write.

Talking about prices

How ¹ _much_ **is** that jacket?	**It's** one thousand pounds!
How much ² _____ those gloves?	**They're** four pounds fifty.
Can I ³ _____ this swimsuit, please?	Yes, of course. Five pounds, please.

too + adjective

It's **They're**	⁴ _____	expensive.

> I love this hat but it's too small.

> And this hat is too big ...

21 🔘 2:36 **Order to make a dialogue. Then listen and check.**

a Nina: Oh! It's too expensive. I've only got twenty pounds. How much are those dark blue jeans? ▢

b Shop assistant: Yes, of course. Eight pounds, please. `8`

c Nina: Great. Can I buy it, please? ▢

d Shop assistant: They're eighteen pounds fifty. ▢

e Nina: Well, they're cheap but they're too baggy. I like wearing tight jeans. How much is that scarf? ▢

f Shop assistant: The jumper's twenty-one pounds. ▢

g Nina: Excuse me. How much is that jumper? `1`

h Shop assistant: It's eight pounds. ▢

22 🔘 2:37 **Listen again and tick (✓) the true sentences.**

1 The jumper is too expensive. ✓
2 Nina has got twenty-one pounds. ▢
3 The jeans are dark blue and tight. ▢
4 The jeans are dark blue, baggy and cheap. ▢
5 The scarf is eighteen pounds fifty. ▢
6 Nina buys the scarf. ▢

23 **Read and write.**

- Write about your clothes.
- Use: *My favourite . . . is/are . . .; It/They . . .; I don't like my . . . because it's/they're too . . .*

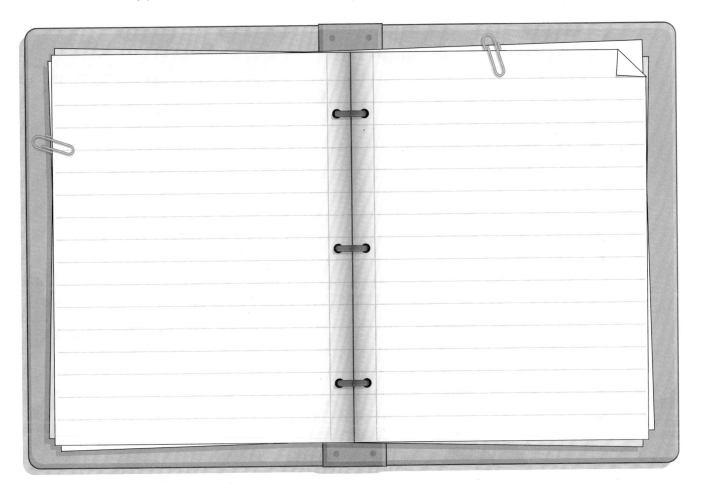

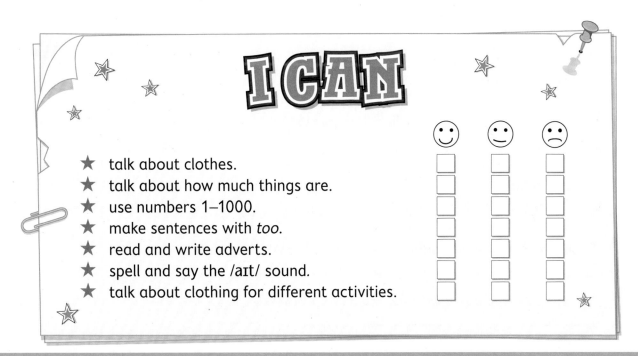

★ talk about clothes.
★ talk about how much things are.
★ use numbers 1–1000.
★ make sentences with *too*.
★ read and write adverts.
★ spell and say the /aɪt/ sound.
★ talk about clothing for different activities.

6 Party time

1 Complete the words. Then look and write the names.

Hi, I'm Dan and this is my family

1 Martin and Becky are my p _a_ _r_ _e_ n t s.
2 Saskia and her brother, Ollie, are my c __ __ s __ n s.
3 Caroline is my a __ __ t.
4 Andy is my u __ c l __.
5 Sue and John are my g r __ __ d p __ __ e n t s.
6 Ollie is a b __ b__.

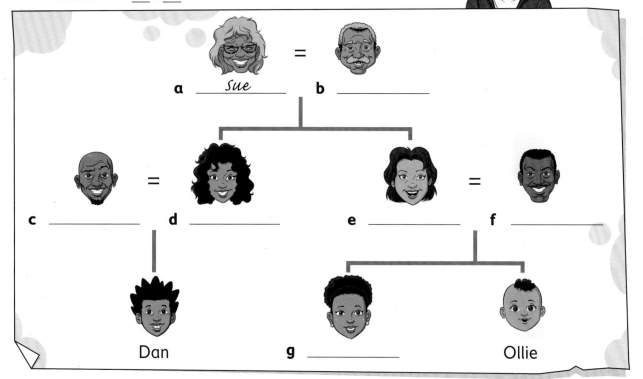

a _Sue_   b _____

c _____   d _____   e _____   f _____

Dan   g _____   Ollie

2 Read and write.

1 Caroline and Andy are Ollie's _____ _parents._ _____
2 Becky is Saskia's _____.
3 Martin is Ollie's _____.
4 Dan is Saskia's _____.
5 Sue and John are Ollie's _____.

3 Write about your family in your notebook.

I've got two parents. I haven't got a brother.

4 **Read and write *was* or *were*.**

1 Yesterday ___*was*___ Dan's birthday. ☑
2 He _____ thirteen. ☐
3 The party _____ fun. ☐
4 His cousins _____ at the party. ☐
5 There _____ some games in the garden. ☐
6 He _____ wet after the games. ☐
7 There _____ a blue birthday cake. ☐

5 (2:43) **Listen and tick (✓) the true sentences in Activity 4.**

6 **Look and read. Write *R* (Robbie) or *E* (Emma).**

Robbie's party in February

Emma's party in July

1 It was sunny.   *E*
2 There were seven children. ☐
3 There was a big cake.   ☐

4 Maddy was at the party. ☐
5 There was music.   ☐
6 There were drinks.   ☐

7 **What was good about the parties? Write sentences in your notebook.**

Emma's party was good because it was sunny.

8 (2:47) Listen and match.

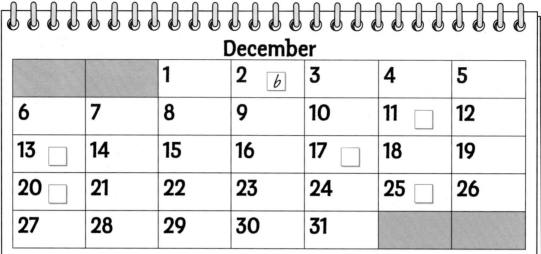

9 Look at Activity 8. Read and write *said* or *went*, and the date.

1 Annabel __went__ to a party at school _____on 20th December_____ .
2 She _____, 'Happy Christmas!' _____ .
3 She _____, 'Happy Birthday!' to her mum _____ .
4 She _____, 'Happy Birthday!' to her cousin _____ .
5 She _____ to her football club party _____ .
6 She _____ to a dance show _____ .

10 Write about events from last month in your notebook.

It was my aunt's birthday on 12th April. We went to the zoo.

11 2:49 **Look and write _ph_ or _th_. Then listen and say.**

My ¹*th*irteen__ ²bir__day
was on ³__ursday.

I've got a ⁴__oto of a
⁵dol__in on my ⁶__one.

⁷Ele__ants are ⁸heal__y
but they aren't very ⁹__in.

12 2:50 **Listen and choose.**

The party was:
a at the beach.
b at school.

13 2:51 **Listen again and complete
for Lucy.**

	Lucy	Me
What was the weather like?	¹ _sunny_ and ² _____	
Where was the party?	at the ³ _____	
What food was there?	⁴ _____, salad and strawberries	
What games were there?	⁵ _____	
Was there any dancing?	no	
Was there any singing?	⁶ _____	

14 **Imagine you went to a party yesterday. Complete the table in Activity 13
for you. Then write in your notebook.**

Sunday, 17th August
Yesterday, I went to a fantastic party on a boat on the river. It was hot and sunny.

15 **Number the sentences in order.**

a   Jenny and Finn got in the snowmobile. ☐

b   The thieves were in a boat. ☐

c   The thieves went into a cave in the sea. ☐

d   The thieves went into a shop. *1*

e   The children went to Snow Mountain. ☐

STORY

16 **Read and draw.**

There was a mountain next to the sea. It was snowy. There were two penguins in the sea. There was a statue of a man at the top of the mountain. There was a big cave in the mountain. The boat was in the cave. The boat was small and red. Rufus and Ivan were in the boat.

17 **Look at page 8. Find and write.**

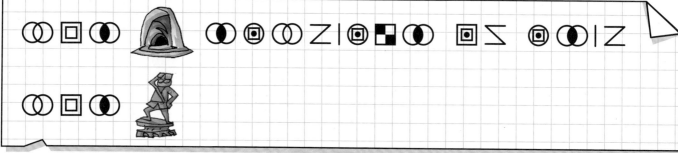

18 Imagine you are on the *Mayflower*. Circle six things for your new life.

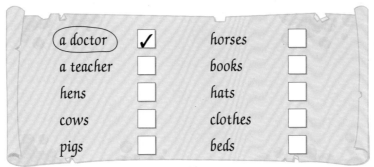

(a doctor)	✓	horses	☐
a teacher	☐	books	☐
hens	☐	hats	☐
cows	☐	clothes	☐
pigs	☐	beds	☐

19 (2:54) Listen and tick (✓) the things that were on the *Mayflower*.

20 (2:55) Read and write. Then listen and check.

was (x 2)   were (x 2)   said   went

My Journal, by Samuel Payne

25th December 1661

Our first months here ¹___were___ very bad. My parents
²_____ very thin because there was no food. I ³_____
thin, too. We were very scared.

In the summer, I often ⁴_____ to the river with my Native
American friends. I ⁵_____ good at fishing! Then, in the
autumn, there was a big Thanksgiving party. We ⁶_____,
'Thank you' to the Native Americans for their help.

21 Look and write the rest of Samuel's journal in your notebook.

ninety Native Americans   fifty settlers   meat   fish from the river
vegetables from our farm   songs and games   'Goodbye'

At the party, there were ninety Native Americans and …

22 Read and write.

Talking about the past

I ¹ _was_ at a party.
You ² _____ happy.
He/She/It ³ _____ great.
We ⁴ _____ at school.
They ⁵ _____ at the river.

There ⁶ _____ a disco.
There ⁷ _____ some people.

I
You
He/She/It
We
They

went to a party.

said, 'Hello.'

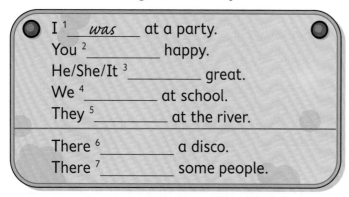

> I went to the shops on my skateboard yesterday.

Ordinal numbers

1st	first	11th	eleventh	21st	twenty-first
2nd	second	12th	twelfth	22nd	twenty-second
3rd	third	13th	thirteenth	23rd	twenty-third
4th	fourth	14th	fourteenth	24th	twenty-fourth
5th	fifth	15th	fifteenth	25th	twenty-fifth
6th	sixth	16th	sixteenth	26th	twenty-sixth
7th	seventh	17th	seventeenth	27th	twenty-seventh
8th	eighth	18th	eighteenth	28th	twenty-eighth
9th	ninth	19th	nineteenth	29th	twenty-ninth
10th	tenth	20th	twentieth	30th	thirtieth
				31st	thirty-first

23 (2:56) Read and choose. Then listen and check.

Yesterday, I ¹**were / went** to a party. My favourite film stars, Keira Philips and Johnny Jones, ²**was / went** to the party, too. I ³**said / was**, 'Hello.' Keira ⁴**was / were** kind and Johnny ⁵**was / were** very funny. There ⁶**was / were** some other nice people, too. We ⁷**was / were** very tired after the party but it ⁸**was / went** a fantastic day!

 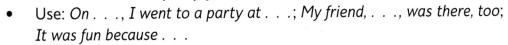

24 **Read and write.**

- Write about a fun party you went to.
- Use: *On . . ., I went to a party at . . .; My friend, . . ., was there, too; It was fun because . . .*
- Ask a friend and write about his/her party.

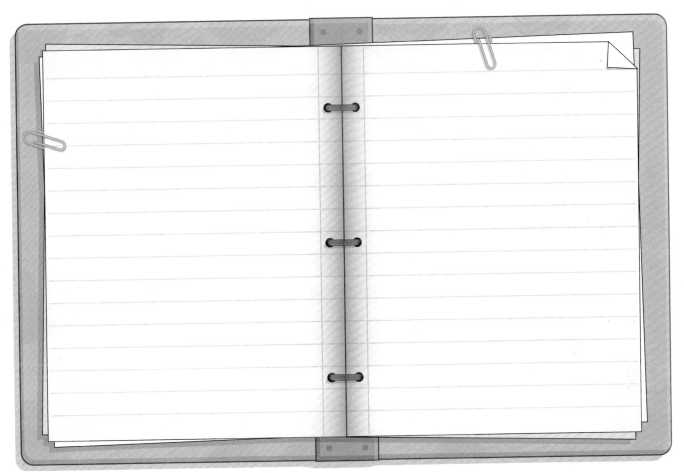

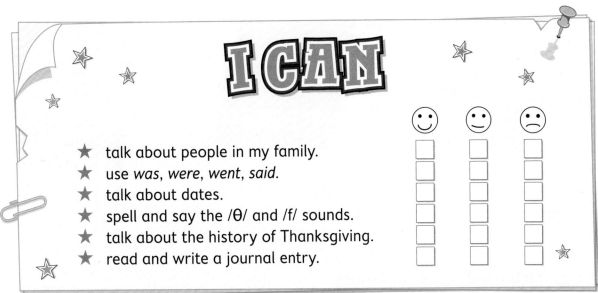

I CAN

	☺	☺	☹
★ talk about people in my family.	☐	☐	☐
★ use *was, were, went, said*.	☐	☐	☐
★ talk about dates.	☐	☐	☐
★ spell and say the /θ/ and /f/ sounds.	☐	☐	☐
★ talk about the history of Thanksgiving.	☐	☐	☐
★ read and write a journal entry.	☐	☐	☐

7 School

1 Complete the words.

1 The first lesson at school was e _a_ _s_ y.
2 The second and third lessons were d __ __ f __ c __ __ t.
3 There was an e x __ __ t __ n __ game in the fourth lesson.
4 Lunch was b __ r __ __ g.
5 The lessons after lunch were i n __ __ r __ __ t __ __ __.
6 There was a s c __ __ __ story in the last lesson.

2 Look and write for you. Use words from Activity 1.

You: _____
Maddy: _easy_

You: _____
Maddy: _____

You: _____
Maddy: _____

You: _____
Maddy: _____

You: _____
Maddy: _____

You: _____
Maddy: _____

3 Listen and write for Maddy.

4 **Read. Then match.**

My first day at school was scary. I was only four and there were a lot of big children in the school. The lessons were very difficult. My teacher was kind but I was very sad!

1　Was Emma's first day at school scary?　　　**a**　No, she wasn't.
2　Was she five?　　　**b**　Yes, he was.
3　Were there a lot of big children?　　　**c**　Yes, it was.
4　Were the lessons easy?　　　**d**　No, they weren't.
5　Was her teacher kind?　　　**e**　Yes, she was.
6　Was she sad?　　　**f**　Yes, there were.

5 **Find and write questions about your first day at school. Then write the answers.**

1　(you) (how) (were) (old)

How old were you?
I was

2　(your) (kind) (was) (teacher)

3　(the) (difficult) (lessons) (were)

4　(you) (were) (happy)

6 **Write about the first time you did your favourite sport in your notebook.**

- How old were you?
- Where were you?
- Was it scary/exciting/easy/difficult?

- Who was with you?
- Were you happy?

The first time I played tennis, I was six years old. I was …

7 Find and circle six words. Then find and write the answer.

EGEOGRAPHYNGPESCIENCELMATHSARTISHHISTORY

What was your favourite subject last year?

E _____

8 🔊 3:09 Look and write. Then listen and choose. *True* or *false*?

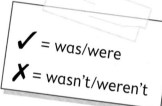

✓ = was/were

✗ = wasn't/weren't

Last week . . .

1 ⚽ + 🌐 ✓ boring _____PE and Geography were boring.____ True / (False)

2 🌐 ✗ easy _____ True / False

3 🎭 ✓ fun _____ True / False

4 🔢 ✗ interesting _____ True / False

5 🧪 + 🔢 ✗ difficult _____ True / False

6 🎨 ✓ exciting _____ True / False

9 Write about your lessons last week in your notebook.

Science wasn't difficult. It was interesting, too.

10 (3:11) **Listen and read. Write the apostrophes (').**

'I can't do my Science homework,' I said to my parents yesterday. 'Can you help?'
'Sorry!' said Dad. 'I havent got time. Ask your sisters.'
'They arent here,' I said.
'Your dad hasnt got time because he doesnt know the answers,' said Mum.
'He wasnt very good at Science at school. But I can help. Science is easy.'
'Thanks, Mum. This is the homework,' I said.
After a long time, Mum said, 'I dont understand. There werent any questions about those things in my Science lessons. Maybe Science isnt easy!'

11 (3:12) **Listen. Where was Suzy's school trip?**

12 (3:13) **Listen again and choose.**

1. Suzy's school trip was (on Thursday) / **yesterday**.
2. There were some beautiful **statues** / **houses**.
3. It was **an Art** / **a Geography** trip.
4. It was a very **interesting** / **boring** day.
5. The children were **excited** / **tired** after the trip.
6. There weren't any **buses** / **trains** in the afternoon.

13 **Read and write about your last school trip.**

My class went on a school trip (when?)_____. It was
(what subject?)_____ trip. We went to (where?)_____.
It was very (boring/interesting/exciting?)_____.

14 **Read and write.**

~~cave~~   got   see   Geography   isn't   too   thieves

1   Where's the _____cave_____ ?
2   I can't _____ it! It _____ here.
3   You're good at _____ .
4   Look, the _____ !
5   We've _____ the treasure.
6   We're _____ late!

15 **Look and write.**

16 **Look at page 8. Find and write.**

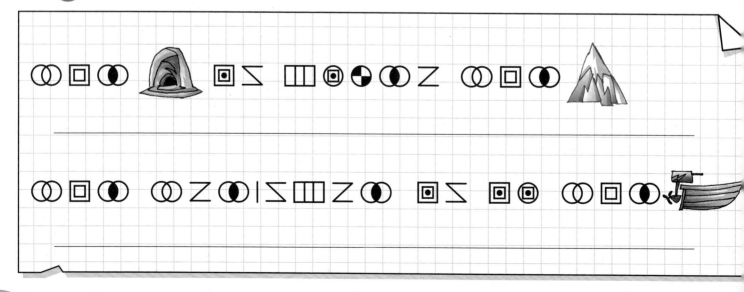

17 Look and write questions. Then answer for Tara.

1 any other children/on your farm ✗
_____Were there any other children on your farm?_____ _____No, there weren't._____

2 any horses/on your farm ✓
_____ _____

3 a radio/in your house ✓
_____ _____

4 a TV/in your house ✗
_____ _____

5 any teachers/near your house ✗
_____ _____

18 3:16 Listen and write.

Star Interview!

And then we went to the USA and I went to ¹___school___ there.
² _____ **you happy at your new school?**
No, I ³_____. It was very ⁴_____ in a class with lots of other children.
⁵_____ **your teachers good?**
Yes, they were. But the ⁶_____ and English lessons were too ⁷_____ and the History and Geography lessons were too ⁸_____.
What was your favourite subject?
⁹_____. I was in the basketball team. It was very ¹⁰_____.
In Australia, there ¹¹_____ any ball sports in PE because there weren't any other children!

19 Write about your first school in your notebook.

My teacher was good. There were a lot of pictures in the classroom.

20 Read and write.

Asking about the past

Was I at school?	Yes, you [1] _were_ .	No, you **weren't**.
Were you at home?	Yes, I **was**.	No, I [2] _____ .
[3] _____ he/she/it happy?	Yes, he/she/it **was**.	No, he/she/it **wasn't**.
Were we tired?	Yes, we **were**.	No, we [4] _____ .
[5] _____ they funny?	Yes, they **were**.	No, they **weren't**.
Was there a cake?	Yes, there **was**.	No, there **wasn't**.
Were there any boys?	Yes, there **were**.	No, there **weren't**.

Talking about the past (negative)

I [6] _____ at the party.
You **weren't** in the kitchen.
He/She/It **wasn't** scary.
We [7] _____ on TV.
They **weren't** sad.

There **wasn't** a cat.
There **weren't** any dogs.

Was I good at Music at school?

Er, yes dear.

21 (3:17) Read and write. Then listen and check.

was (x 3)   were (x 2)   wasn't   weren't

Interviewer: What was your school like, David?
David: My school [1] _was_ a tennis school.
Interviewer: Were there other lessons, too?
David: Yes, there [2] _____ – Maths, Science, English and History. But they [3] _____ only in the morning. There were tennis lessons every afternoon.
Interviewer: [4] _____ it a good school?
David: Yes, it [5] _____ . My sister [6] _____ happy there. Her favourite subject was Art but there [7] _____ any Art teachers at the school. But it was a great school for a tennis player!

22 **Read and write.**

- Write about your favourite subjects last year.
- Use: (*Maths*) *was/wasn't* . . .

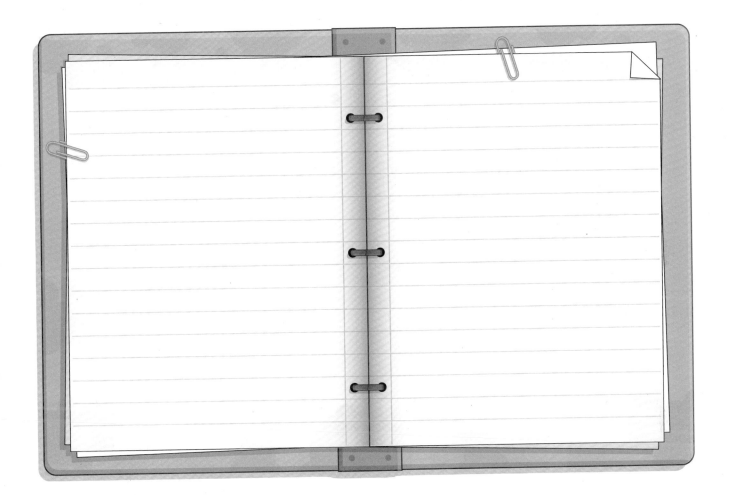

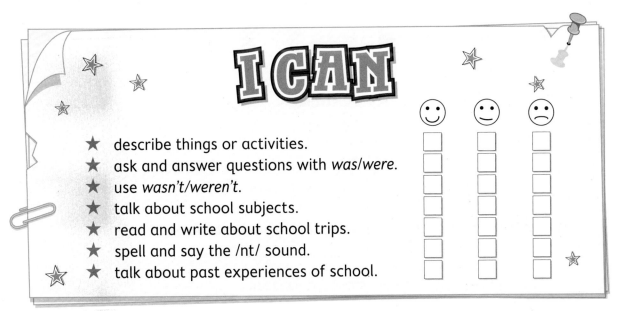

I CAN

	😊	🙂	☹️
★ describe things or activities.	☐	☐	☐
★ ask and answer questions with *was/were*.	☐	☐	☐
★ use *wasn't/weren't*.	☐	☐	☐
★ talk about school subjects.	☐	☐	☐
★ read and write about school trips.	☐	☐	☐
★ spell and say the /nt/ sound.	☐	☐	☐
★ talk about past experiences of school.	☐	☐	☐

1 Look and write. Then complete the crossword.

1 Japan → *Japanese*
2 the USA → _____
3 Mexico → _____
4 Spain → _____
5 Australia → _____
6 Britain → _____
7 China → _____
8 Brazil → _____
9 Egypt → _____
10 Argentina → _____
11 India → _____
12 Italy → _____

2 🔊 3:21 Listen and match.

1	Nicole Kidman	Spain	football player
2	J.K. Rowling	Australia	writer
3	Rafael Nadal	the USA	singer
4	Lionel Messi	Argentina	tennis player
5	Beyoncé	Britain	actress

3 Write about the people in Activity 2 in your notebook.

1 Nicole Kidman is an Australian actress.

4 Read and write the years in numbers and in words.

> Last year, it was 2010 (twenty ten).

1 Last year, it was _____ (_____).
2 Two years ago, it was _____ (_____).
3 Ten years ago, it was _____ (_____).
4 Fifty years ago, it was _____ (_____).

5 (3:23) Listen and write.

Name: **Will Smith**
Nationality: American
Job: singer and actor
¹ _1986_ : first successful song
² _____ : first TV programme
³ _____ : first film
⁴ _____ : first film with one of his children

Will Smith

6 Imagine you are famous and write.

Name: _____
Nationality: _____
Job: _____
2010: _____
2028: _____
2029: _____
1st October 2030: _____
24th November 2030: _____

7 Look at Activity 6. Imagine it is 1st December 2030. Write sentences using *last* or *ago* in your notebook.

> Last week, I went to China.
> Two years ago, I was in my first Real Madrid match.

8 Find and circle twelve jobs. Then write.

1

2

spy

c	o	w	b	o	y	s	w	o	i	h
d	s	a	n	t	e	a	c	h	e	r
e	o	i	u	j	r	k	c	j	i	s
y	l	t	r	s	a	i	l	o	r	p
q	d	e	s	d	a	n	c	e	r	y
f	i	r	e	f	i	g	h	t	e	r
u	e	s	f	b	z	e	r	e	f	n
l	r	a	s	t	r	o	n	a	u	t
s	c	i	e	n	t	i	s	t	x	n

3

4

5

6

7

8

9

10

11

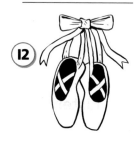
12

9 Look and complete.

~~Saturday~~   half past three   the winter   December   night
the afternoon   seven o'clock   25th August   1995   Tuesday

in	on	at
	Saturday	

10 (3:27) **Read and write. Then listen, check and say.**

1   A _____swimmer_____ can swim.
2   A _____ can dance.
3   An actor can _____.

4   A _____ can sail.
5   A _____ can sing.
6   A teacher can _____.

11 (3:28) **Read. Then listen and number.**

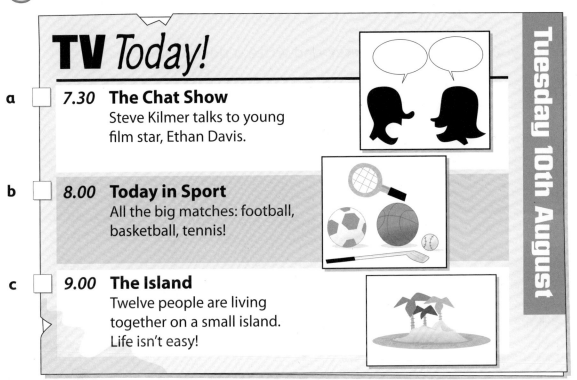

TV *Today!*

a ☐ *7.30* **The Chat Show**
Steve Kilmer talks to young
film star, Ethan Davis.

b ☐ *8.00* **Today in Sport**
All the big matches: football,
basketball, tennis!

c ☐ *9.00* **The Island**
Twelve people are living
together on a small island.
Life isn't easy!

Tuesday 10th August

12 (3:29) **Listen again and write.**

1   The tennis match is very ___exciting___.
2   The players in the match are Spanish and _____.
3   The film star was a _____ in his first film.
4   The film star's birthday was _____ weeks ago.
5   On the island, there isn't any _____.
6   There was rain on the island three _____ ago.

13 **Write about your favourite TV or radio programme in your notebook.**

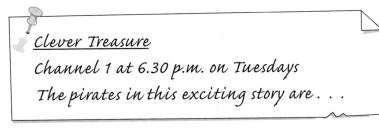

Clever Treasure
Channel 1 at 6.30 p.m. on Tuesdays
The pirates in this exciting story are . . .

14 **Read and match.**

1 How does Rufus feel in Picture 1?   **a** Jenny
2 What does the penguin do?   **b** Captain Formosa
3 How do Rufus and Ivan feel in Picture 3? **c** He feels happy.
4 Who arrives in the submarine?   **d** It scares the thieves.
5 What is the statue?   **e** They feel scared.
6 Who says, 'Well done, penguins!'?   **f** It's a golden penguin.

15 **Draw your favourite character and write a description.**

_____

_____

_____

16 **Look at page 8. Find and write.**

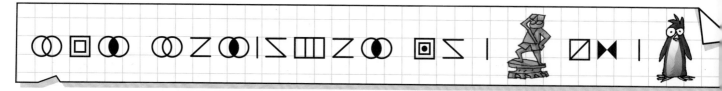

_____

17 (3:32) **Read and circle. Then listen and check.**

¹*In* / *On* / *At* the winter, it's dark after school. I come home ²*in* / *on* / *at* half past three and do my homework. Then, I play computer games. ³*Last* / *Yesterday* / *Three* year, my favourite computer game was *Nintendogs* but now my favourite is *Guitar Hero*. Two months ⁴*last* / *ago* / *then*, I wasn't very good at ⁵*play* / *player* / *playing* the game – some of the music is very difficult – but now I'm a good ⁶*play* / *player* / *playing*. I often play ⁷*in* / *on* / *at* the evening with my friends and ⁸*in* / *on* / *at* Saturdays and Sundays, too.

18 **Read the puzzle and think.**

Four days ago, a cowboy went to the city on Friday. Yesterday, he went home on Friday. How?

19 **Read and circle. *True* (✓) or *false* (✗)? Then find and write the answer.**

Technology Quiz...

		✓	✗
1	There were computer games a hundred years ago.	✔ We	✗ (The)
2	There were computer games in 1940.	✔ can	✗ horse's
3	Mario is a famous computer game character.	✔ name	✗ act
4	Before the books and films, Harry Potter was a computer game.	✔ in	✗ was
5	In FIFA computer games, you play football.	✔ Friday	✗ films

1 ___*The*___ 2 _____ 3 _____ 4 _____ 5 _____!

20 Read and write.

Talking about times

1 _last_ | week
month
year

two days
six months
ten years | 2 _____

3 _____ | January
the summer
1979

4 _____ | Thursday
1st February

5 _____ | night
half past eight

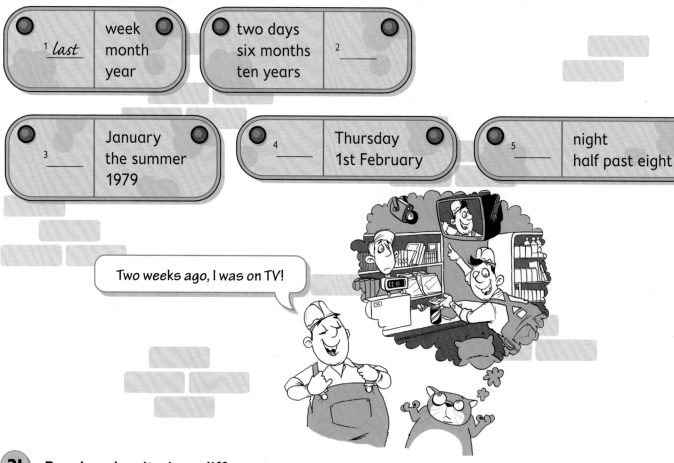

Two weeks ago, I was on TV!

21 Read and write in a different way.

1 His film was very successful in 2010. (It's now 2011.)

His film was very successful last year.

2 That was my favourite computer game in July. (It's now September.)

_____

3 The programme was on TV two days ago. (It's now Wednesday.)

_____

4 She was on the radio on 2nd February. (It's now 9th February.)

_____

5 My dad was a singer twelve years ago. (It's now 2015.)

_____

6 We were in Hollywood three months ago. (It's now November.)

_____

7 I went to the supermarket yesterday. (It's now 5th July.)

_____

8 Steve went to bed two hours ago. (It's now eleven o'clock.)

_____

22 **Read and write.**

- Write about your favourite entertainment.
- Use: *I listen to . . .; I watch . . .; I play it on/at . . .*

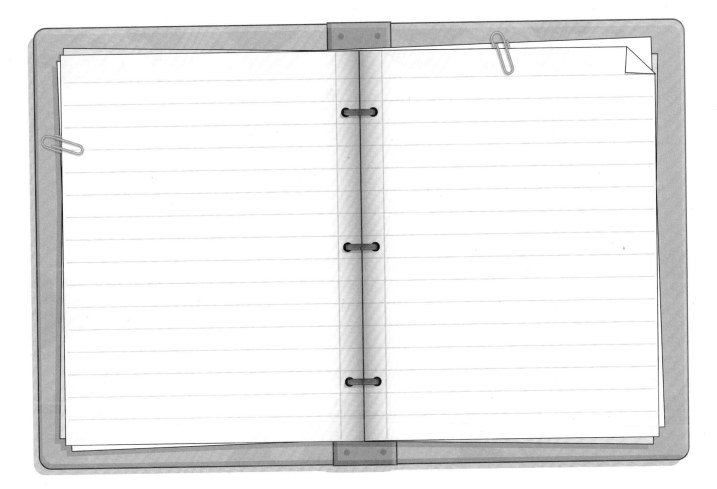

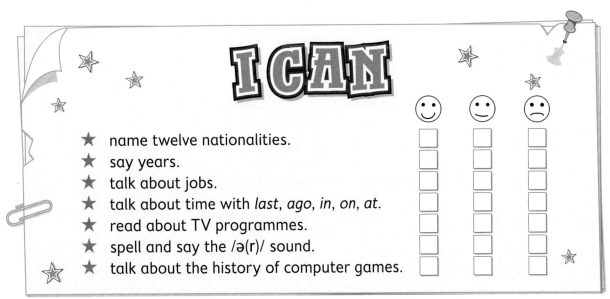

I CAN

	☺	😐	☹
★ name twelve nationalities.	☐	☐	☐
★ say years.	☐	☐	☐
★ talk about jobs.	☐	☐	☐
★ talk about time with *last, ago, in, on, at*.	☐	☐	☐
★ read about TV programmes.	☐	☐	☐
★ spell and say the /ə(r)/ sound.	☐	☐	☐
★ talk about the history of computer games.	☐	☐	☐

Thanksgiving

1 Complete the crossword.

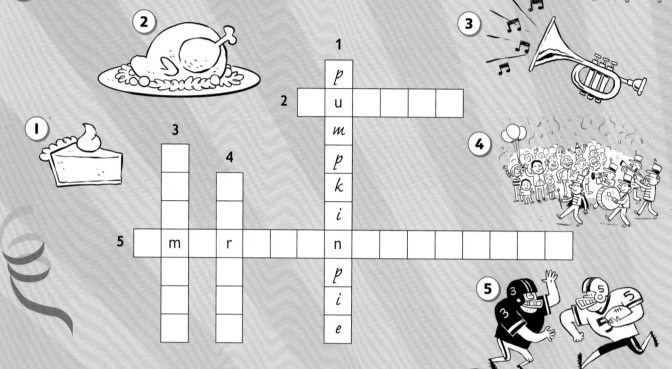

		1
		p
2	p u				
		m
3		p
	4	k
		i
5	m	r		n							
		p
		i
		e

2 🔊 3:34 Read and tick (✓). Then listen and check.

1 Thanksgiving is in:

a  ☐   b  ✓

2 Children don't go to school on:

a  ☐   b  ☐

3 Charlie plays the:

a  ☐   b  ☐

4 People usually eat:

a  ☐   b  ☐

Christmas

1 Look. Then find and write.

1

epesrstn
presents

2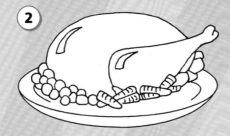

tykreu
_____

3

slssurBe tssprou
_____

4

ingtocks
_____

5

nStaa lsuCa
_____

6

ddgpuin
_____

2 (3:36) Listen and complete.

	Present 1	Present 2	Present 3
brother	_ball_		
sister			
grandad			

Word list

1
Friends

artist
bald
beautiful
bossy
clever
cool
curly
emergency
good-looking
kind
lazy
map
message
penguins
shy
spiky
sporty
straight
submarine
warm

What **does** she **look like**?
What **do** they **look like**?
She**'s**/They**'re** beautiful.
She**'s**/They**'ve got** blond hair.
You're sporty **and** you're clever.
You're bossy **but** I don't mind.
I like you **because** you're kind.

2
My life

after
afternoon
always
before
bones
brush my teeth
do my homework
energy
escaping
evening
make my bed
meet my friends
never
often
sometimes
tidy my room
treasure
usually
wash my face

He does **his** homework.
She washes **her** face.
It washes **its** head.
We brush **our** teeth.
They brush **their** hair.

3
Free time

acting
be careful
catching
climbing
dangerous
diving
drawing
hitting
instruments
kicking
piano
playing chess
playing the drums
polar bears
rollerblading
skateboarding
thieves
throwing
trampolining
trumpet
violins

I**'m**/You**'re good at** throw**ing**.
She **isn't good at** danc**ing**.
They **aren't good at** climb**ing**.
What do you **like** do**ing**?
What **are** you **good at**?
He/She **loves** skateboard**ing**.
They **like** act**ing**.

4
Around the world

Argentina
Australia
Brazil
Britain
cave
China
city
desert
Egypt
forest
Greenland
holiday
Italy
lake
Mexico
pyramid
remember
Spain
statue
the USA
volcano

There**'s a** competition.
There **isn't a** competition.
There **are some**/ **aren't any** snakes.
Is there **a** desert?
Are there **any** volcanoes?
Yes, there **is**/**are**./ No, there **isn't**/ **aren't**.

5
Shopping

baggy
bend
cheap
dark
expensive
gloves
jacket
light
middle
pounds
rock climbing
sandals
scarf
soft
soles
stiff
sunglasses
swimsuit
tight

How much is that scarf?
It's two pounds fifty.
How much are those gloves?
They're fifteen pounds.
Can I buy this jacket, please?
It**'s**/They**'re too** expensive.

6
Party time

aunt
baby
cousin
disco
grandparents
Native Americans
need
North America
parents
settlers
South Africa
Thanksgiving
uncle

first
second
third
fourth
fifth
sixth
seventh
eighth
ninth
tenth

I **was** very hungry.
The cars **were** small.
I **said**, 'Happy New Year!'
I **went** to a party.

7
School

Art
boring
difficult
easy
exciting
Geography
interesting
kilometres
Maths
PE
History
radio
scary
Science

Was it scary?
Yes, it **was**./No, it **wasn't**.
Were they the winners?
Yes, they **were**./
No, they **weren't**.
Was there an alien in it?
Yes, there **was**./
No, there **wasn't**.
Were there any children in the story?
Yes, there **were**./
No, there **weren't**.
Last year, Maths **wasn't** easy.
The lessons **weren't** fun.

8
Entertainment

American
Argentinian
Australian
autograph
Brazilian
British
Chinese
cowboy
Egyptian
golden
grandfather
Indian
Italian
Japanese
king
Mexican
restaurant
rich
sailor
scientist
soldier
Spanish
spy
successful
table tennis
waiter

She was in a film two days **ago**.
He was in a Spanish team **last** week.
in the morning
on Thursday
at five o'clock

Wider World

Families of the world
argue
dirty
help
husband
practice
washing
  machines

Funny sports
cheese rolling
elephant polo
hill
mud racing
reindeer
  racing
sticks
winner

Shopping for food
bakery
coconuts
floating
grow
seeds

Unusual schools
boarding school
international
Japanese
skier
snowboarding
the Olympics

Festival

Thanksgiving
American
  football
colourful
mashed
  potato
parade
pumpkin pie
trumpet
turkey

Christmas
Brussels
  sprouts
presents
pudding
Santa Claus
stocking
turkey